DINOSAUR COLORING BOOK

FOR KIDS AGES 4-8

THIS BOOK BELONGS TO

PARASAUROLOPHUS

ANKYLOSAURUS

TRICERATOPS

BRACHIOSAURUS

TRICERATOPS TIME!

BRACHIOSAURUS

VOLCANO

T-REX ADVENTURE

DINO TIME

PACHYCEPHALOS AURUS

PTERODACTYL

T-REX

STEGOSAURUS

BRACHIOSAURUS

VELOCIRAPTOR

CARNOTAURUS

DIPLODOCUS

BABY TRICERATOPS

PTERODACTYL

DINO FAMILY

VELOCIRAPTOR BUTTERFLY

BRONTOSAURUS

BABY DINO

ROAR!

STEGOSAURUS

RAPTORS

CARNOTAURUS

CHARGE!

PTERANODON

STOMP!

DINOSAUR DAY!

SPEED!

SWIMMING

DISCOVER!

COOL

FLY

BALL

HERO!

CHRISTMAS

EASTER

SUMMER

FUN

PIRATE

BIRTHDAY

SKY

VELOCIRAPTORS

TRICERATOPS

FLYING

STAR

Made in United States
Troutdale, OR
11/24/2024

25259512R00035